WHY DO WE NEED TREES?

Olivia Watson

Illustrated by Tjarda Borsboom

First published in 2024 by Hungry Tomato Ltd
F15, Old Bakery Studios, Blewetts Wharf, Malpas Road, Truro, Cornwall, TR1 1QH, UK.

A CIP catalog record for this book is available from the British Library.

ISBN 9781916598997

Printed in China

Discover more at
www.hungrytomato.com

Picture Credits

Abbreviations: m-middle, t-top, l-left, r-right, bg-background.

Shutterstock: Andrey_Kuzmin 19br; franconiaphoto 21ml; Kalcutta 23tr; Karuna Eberl 23ml; Loreanto 19tl; Maishkoff 20ml; Mazur Travel 21t; M.Schuppich 23ml; nnattalli 23mr; Sweet Momento Photography 23mr; Rawpixel.com 18tl, 18mr; Vova Shevchuk 23tl.

Every effort has been made to trace the copyright holders, and we apologize in advance for any unintentional omissions. We would be pleased to insert the appropriate acknowledgments in any subsequent edition of this publication.

Contents

Words in **BOLD** can be found in the glossary.

What Is a Tree?

Trees are living things that can be found almost everywhere on Earth! They are important for people and nature. Trees come in all shapes and sizes, but most have the same four parts.

Some trees have other features, such as fruit, which are full of hidden seeds. Some are tiny, like apple seeds, and some are much bigger, like avocado seeds.

Not a tree

Some plants that we call trees aren't trees at all! Cacti and boojum aren't made of wood, and palms don't have branches, so they don't count!

Trees and Me

Your home is probably filled with things that are made from trees.

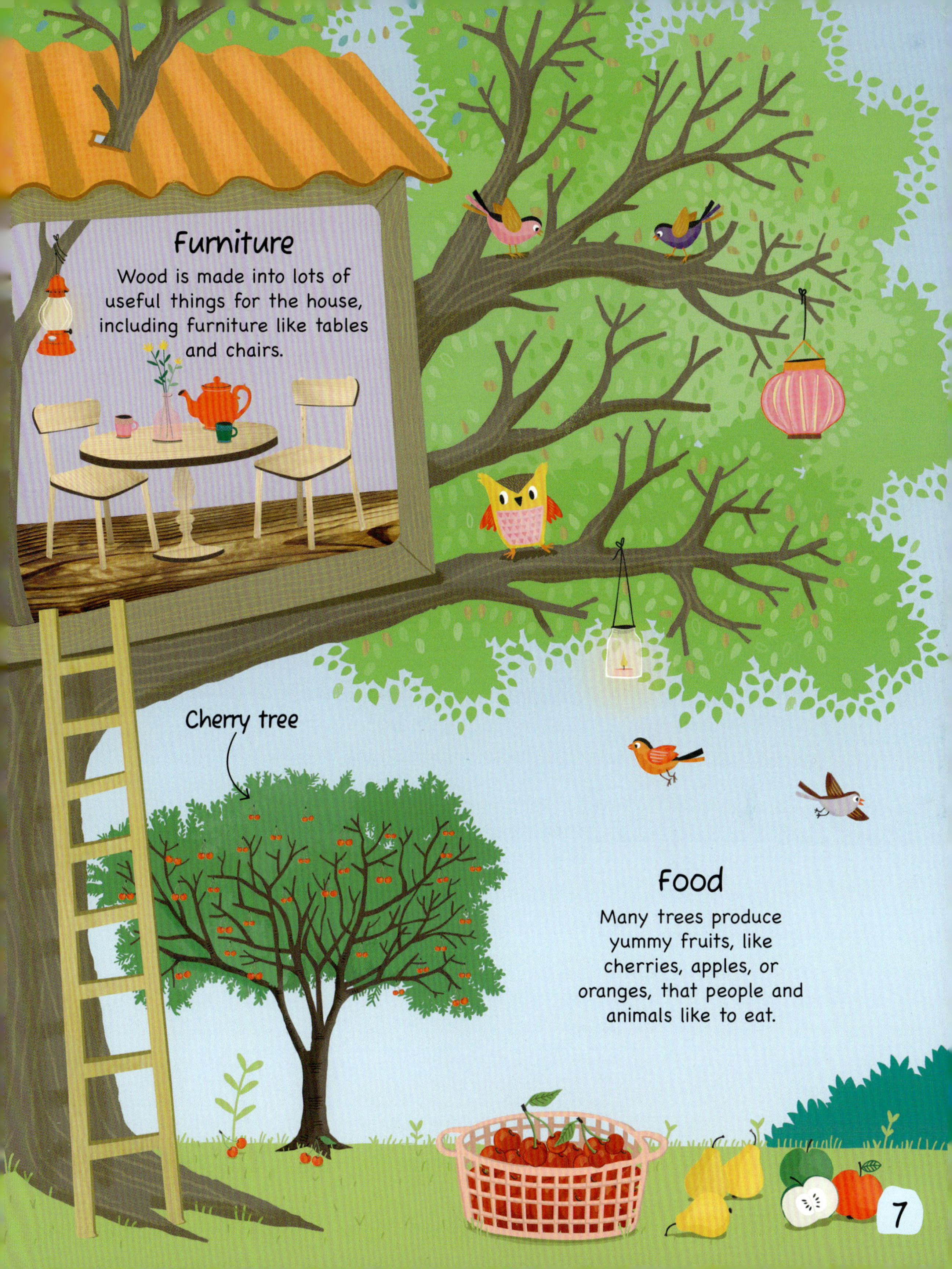

Furniture

Wood is made into lots of useful things for the house, including furniture like tables and chairs.

Cherry tree

Food

Many trees produce yummy fruits, like cherries, apples, or oranges, that people and animals like to eat.

Good and Bad

Some trees have healing powers and have been used in medicines for centuries, but others are deadly!

Alder tree

The **bark** from this tree can be turned into a medicinal tea that helps soothe sore throats.

Manchineel

Also called "death apple tree"! The leaves give a nasty burn, and eating the fruit can be deadly.

Apple tree

Eating fruit helps keep us healthy. Apples are good for our stomachs and hearts, and they help us to avoid illness.

Elder tree

Lots of parts of the elder tree can be used in medicines, like the flowers, which help treat fevers, colds, and flu.

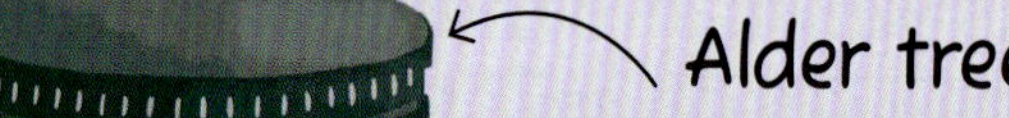

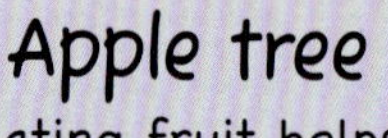

Spindle tree
With bright fruit and seeds, the spindle tree may look pretty, but it's poisonous to humans and many animals!

Strychnine
This tree contains a powerful poison. Once used in medicine in tiny amounts, it's now thought to be dangerous and not used much anymore!

Willow bark
Willow tree bark has been used as a natural painkiller for more than 3,500 years!

9

Animal Homes

Lots of different animals around the world make their homes in and around trees.

Branch adventurers

Monkeys live in the treetops, using their strong arms or tails to swing from branch to branch in search of food.

Dam builders

Using strong teeth, beavers chew through tree trunks for wood to build their dams and special shelters called "lodges".

Leafy living

Some animals, like sloths, live in trees, using the leaves to hide from the bigger animals that hunt them.

Safety nest

Many birds build nests high in the trees to keep their babies away from animals that would try to eat them!

Hollow hideaways

Small animals live inside tree hollows where they're hidden and safe.

Beaver lodge

11

Wildlife Homes

Even the smallest creatures use trees for food and shelter, from up in the top branches to down on the ground.

Insect central

From butterflies eating **nectar** to beetles burrowing into fallen logs, trees are home to many insects.

Shady plants

It's not just animals; lots of plants can be found around trees, making the most of the shelter they provide.

Sneaky reptiles

Some crafty snakes and lizards are good at blending in with trees and can sneak up and catch other animals!

Let's Make a Wildlife Log House
Create a home for insects using nature finds!

You will need:

- Big pieces of wood
- Big logs
- Twigs
- Moss
- Leaves
- Cones

Important information:

When collecting natural materials, always ask permission and only take things that have fallen to the ground; don't break branches off trees or damage plants!

1. Adventure into a nearby woods to collect pieces of wood and logs. Always go with an adult to stay safe.

2. In your yard, place two logs upright, leaving space in between. Ask an adult to secure them into the ground.

3. Pile the rest of the logs and wood as shown. You may need to collect more if they don't fill the space!

4. Collect smaller natural materials such as moss, twigs, leaves, and cones. Insects love all of these!

5. Use these to fill in any gaps and finish the log house. Check back daily to see which insects you can spot!

Healthy Planet

Trees play an important part in keeping our planet happy and healthy. We have a lot to thank them for!

Pollution preventer

Tree roots act like sponges. They help to keep water clean by soaking up the things that could **pollute** it.

$$O^2$$

Happy habitats

Woods provide a great place for us to go and study nature, play, and have fun!

Global warming

Too much carbon dioxide can lead to **global warming**! Planting more trees will help to stop that from happening.

Let's Plant a Tree

Help the planet by planting your very own tree! Choosing the perfect planting place will help your tree to grow.

You will need:

- Tree sapling
- Shovel
- Watering can
- Stake/cane (to hold the tree upright)
- String

Where to plant

Some places have rules on planting trees, and some trees grow to be gigantic, so make sure an adult checks that your chosen spot is okay.

Choosing your tree

Choose a tree that's **native** to your area. It will be used to the weather and soil, and find it easier to grow!

Time to plant!

Tree planting seasons vary – ask your local plant nursery for the best time to buy and plant your sapling.

1.

Ask an adult to cut the grass and pull up any weeds in the area you'll be planting your tree.

2.

Dig a hole deep enough for all the roots to fit in and twice as wide. Keep the soil close – you'll need it again soon.

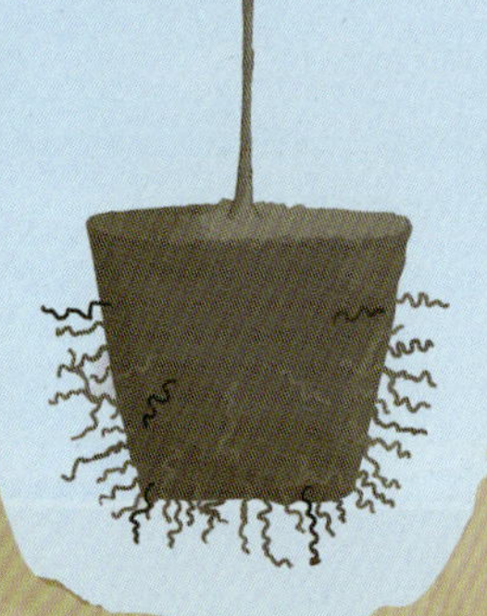

3.

It's important that the sapling goes into a level hole, otherwise it won't grow properly!

4.

Place your sapling in the hole, making sure it fits inside comfortably and is standing up straight.

5.

Using the dug soil, refill the hole, making sure to cover all the roots. Press down around the trunk so that it's secure in the ground.

6.

Push your stake/cane 2 feet (60 cm) into the soil. Tie the sapling to it with string. This will help it stay upright, even in windy weather.

7.

Water the soil around your sapling to make it moist. It shouldn't need watering much after this; its roots will find water in the soil themselves.

8.

Trees grow at different speeds: some take 2–10 years and others take more than 30 to reach full size! Keep the area free from weeds and pests to help your tree grow. After 2–3 years, most trees should stand without the stake/cane.

Protecting Trees

Trees do so much good for the world; it's important that we protect them. There are lots of easy things we can do to help.

Planting plants and trees

Growing your own trees at home – if you can – means there will be more trees in the world to carry out their amazing jobs, like cleaning the air and water.

Reducing waste and recycling

Re-using, recycling and choosing to buy things made from recycled materials all reduce the need for more trees to be cut down.

Cleaning events

Trees are much happier in clean environments. You can help by taking part in local cleaning events, always putting your litter in the correct bin and respecting nature.

Saving water

Turning off the tap when you brush your teeth and taking quicker showers are two easy ways of saving water. This is great for the environment and helps both plants and animals.

Learning more...

Talk to friends and family about the amazing things that trees do for us. Spread the message and encourage them to do their part to help, too!

Did You Know?

Trees are pretty amazing! Every living creature needs trees to survive; the world wouldn't be the way it is today if we didn't have them. Did you know these amazing facts about trees?

A quarter of the ingredients in modern medicines come from **RAINFOREST PLANTS!**

Trees help control how much **WATER** is in the soil, reducing **flooding** and **drought**.

The rings in **TREE TRUNKS** teach scientists what the weather was like in that place in the past!

APPLE TREES
usually need at least 6 years of growing before they start producing fruit.

Trees can help to reduce noise pollution as they naturally block

SOUND WAVES.

Trees are sometimes called the
"LUNGS OF THE EARTH"
because they filter the air to make it clean for animals and humans to breathe.

Match Up the Pairs

**Can you match up the fact boxes (below) with the correct tree (right)?
Flip back through the book if you need a hint!**

1.

I'm also called the "death apple tree" after my deadly leaves and fruit.

2.

My bark has been used as a painkiller for more than 3,500 years!

3.

Humans turn my deliciously sweet sap into syrup.

4.

My bright fruit and seeds may look pretty, but they're very poisonous!

5.

I have small, dark red fruits that grow in bunches.

6.

My flowers are used in medicines to help treat fevers, colds, and flu.

Cherry tree

Willow tree

Spindle tree

Maple tree

Manchineel tree

Elder tree

Have you matched them all?
Answers can be found on page 24.

Glossary

Bark – the tough outer layer of a woody plant stem or root, such as a tree trunk.

Carbon dioxide – an invisible gas in the air that plants take in to make food and oxygen.

Drought - a long period of dryness, usually caused by lack of rainfall.

Flooding - when large amounts of water overflows into areas of land where it shouldn't be.

Global warming – the rising temperature of the planet, which causes climate change.

Habitat – the natural home of plants and animals.

Native – something that naturally grows or lives in a particular area.

Nectar – a sugary liquid produced by flowers.

Nutrients – substances or ingredients that plants and animals need to live and grow.

Oxygen – an invisible gas in the air that plants produce, and people and animals need to breathe.

Poisonous – something that is very harmful and can cause severe illness or death.

Pollute – (verb) to make dirty or harmful with waste, chemicals, or other substances.

Sap – a watery substance that comes out of a plant or tree.

Answers to Match Up the Pairs

Answers: 1. Manchineel tree, 2. Willow tree, 3. Maple tree, 4. Spindle tree, 5. Cherry tree, 6. Elder tree.